Published simultaneously in 1996 by Exley Publications in
Great Britain, and Exley Giftbooks in the USA.

12 11 10 9 8 7 6 5 4 3 2 1

ISBN 1-85015-697-2

Edited and pictures selected by Helen Exley.
Designed by Pinpoint Design Company.
Picture research by P.A. Goldberg and J.M. Clift, Image Select,
London.
Typeset by Delta, Watford.
Printed in Spain.

Exley Publications Ltd, 16 Chalk Hill, Watford, Herts WD1 4BN, UK.
Exley Giftbooks, 232 Madison Avenue, Suite 1206, NY 10016, USA.

Acknowledgements: The publishers are grateful for permission to reproduce
copyright material. Whilst every effort has been made to trace the copyright holders,
the publishers would be pleased to hear from anyone not here acknowledged.
OGDEN NASH: Reprinted by permission of Curtis Brown Group Ltd., London and
Little, Brown & Co. Inc., New York. ELLEN SUE STERN: from "I Do: Meditations for
Brides". Reprinted by permission of Bantam Doubleday Dell Publishing, New York.
Picture Credits: Exley Publications is grateful to the following individuals and
organizations for permission to reproduce their pictures: Archiv fur Kunst (AKG),
Art Resource (AR), Bridgeman Art Library (BAL), Edimedia (EDM), Scala (SCA).
Whilst every effort has been made to trace copyright holders, we would be happy to
hear from any not here acknowledged. Cover: Albert Edelfeld, BAL; title page:
Brueghel the Younger, BAL; p.6: © 1996 Roy Moyer, Lovers in the Snow II, AR; p.9:
Gustav Klimt, AR; p.10: Steinlein, AR; p.13: Harold von Schmidt, AKG; p.14: © 1996
Eugene Higgins, AR; p.16/17: © 1996: Claude Monet, The Seine at Bougival, AKG;
p.19: © 1996 Alexandre Deineka, EDM; p.20: © 1996 Willi Balendat, caricature, AKG;
p.23: © 1996 Raphael Soyer, The Dancing Lesson, Jewish Museum/AR, NY; p.24:
Egyptian sculpture, AKG; p.27: © 1996 Alexandre Deineka, EDM; p.28: Sven Richard
Bergh, BAL; p.30/31: Egyptian painting, AKG; p.32: © 1996 A. Morbelli, Dream and
Reality, AR; p.34/35: 16th century Persian illustration; p.37: M. Gattenberger,
EDM; p.39: © 1996 Philip Wilson Steer, The Bridge, Etaples, BAL; p.41: Egyptian
painting, SCA; p.42: Jan Miense Molenaer, SCA p.44: Ann Ronan Picture Library;
p.46: Ferdinand von Reznicek, AKG; p.49: Egyptian Statuette, BAL; p.51: Ivan
Scishkin, SCA; p.52: Roll, Bulloz; p.54: © 1996 Timothy Easton, Flowering Apple Tree
and Willow, BAL; p.57: Teniers the Younger, BAL; p.59: © 1996 Roy Hammond, Chris
Beetles Gallery; p.60: 17th century Indian pillowcase, AKG.

THE GIFTS OF
MARRIAGE
THE BEST QUOTATIONS

EDITED BY
HELEN EXLEY

≣EXLEY
NEW YORK • WATFORD, UK

"We are two vines curved to one
another... twined into one stem –
too like and near to discern
the changes of our growing."

WALTER BENTON,
from "Never a Greater Need"

"Marriage is the fusion of two hearts – the union of two lives – the coming together of two tributaries."

PETER MARSHALL

"What greater thing is there for two human souls than to feel that they are joined for life – to strengthen each other in all labour, to rest on each other in all sorrow, to minister to each other in all pain, to be one with each other in silent, unspeakable memories at the moment of the last parting."

GEORGE ELIOT (MARY ANN EVANS) (1819-1880)

"What a happy and holy fashion it is that those who love one another should rest on the same pillow."

NATHANIEL HAWTHORNE (1804-1864)

"Husband and wife come to look alike at last."

OLIVER WENDELL HOLMES (1809-1894)

"In the opinion of the world,
marriage ends all, as it does in a comedy.
The truth is precisely the opposite:
it begins all."

ANNE SOPHIE SWETCHINE (1782-1857)

"There is no more lovely, friendly
and charming relationship,
communion or company than a
good marriage."

MARTIN LUTHER (1483-1546),
from "Table Talk"

"A happy marriage has in it all the
pleasures of friendships, all the enjoyments
of sense and reason –
and indeed all the sweets of life."

JOSEPH ADDISON (1672-1719)

"There is no greater risk, perhaps, than
matrimony, but there is nothing happier
than a happy marriage."

BENJAMIN DISRAELI (1804-1881),
*from a letter to Princess Louise on her engagement
to the Marquess of Lorne*

"None can be eternally united who have
not died for each other."
COVENTRY PATMORE,
from "The Red, the Root and the Flower"

"You can never be happily married
to another until you get a divorce
from yourself.
Successful marriage demands a
certain death to self."
JERRY McCANT

"Love means to commit oneself
without guarantee, to give oneself
completely in the hope that our love
will produce love in the loved person.
Love is an act of faith, and whoever
is of little faith is also of
little love."
ERICH FROMM

"Love is, above all, the gift of
oneself."
JEAN ANOUILH (1910-1987)

"[Love is] born with the pleasure
of looking at each other, it is fed with the
necessity of seeing each other,
it is concluded with the impossibility
of separation!"
JOSÉ MARTÍ (1835-1895)

"Duty does not have to be dull.
Love can make it beautiful and fill it
with life."
ANONYMOUS

"Married couples who love each other
tell each other a thousand things
without talking."
CHINESE PROVERB

"For one human being to love
another: that is perhaps the most
difficult of all our tasks, the ultimate,
the last test and proof, the work for
which all other work is
but preparation."
RAINER MARIA RILKE (1875-1926)

"There is no grief, no sorrow, no despair,
no languor, no dejection, no dismay, no
absence scarcely can there be, for those
who love as we do."

WILLIAM WORDSWORTH (1770-1850)

"Man and wife, a king and queen with one or two subjects, and a few square yards of territory of their own: this, really, is marriage. It is true freedom because it is a true fulfilment, for man, woman, and children."

D.H. LAWRENCE (1885-1930)

"What the world needs is not romantic lovers who are sufficient unto themselves, but husbands and wives who live in communities, relate to other people, carry on useful work and willingly give time and attention to their children."

MARGARET MEAD (1901-1978),
from "Redbook"

"Marriage is three parts love and seven
parts forgiveness of sins."
LANGDON MITCHELL

> "Between a man and his wife nothing
> ought to rule but love."
> WILLIAM PENN (1644-1718)

"A successful marriage requires falling in love many times, always with the same person."

MIGNON McLAUGHLIN

"For five whole years I see her every day, and always think I see her for the first time."

JEAN RACINE (1639-1699)

"People do not marry people, not real ones anyway; they marry what they think the person is; they marry illusions and images.
The exciting adventure of marriage is finding out who the partner really is."

JAMES L. FRAMO, b.1922,
from "Explorations in Marital & Family Therapy"

"A happy marriage is based on discovery. For each delights in the differences in the other – and goes on learning all life long."

PAM BROWN, b.1928

"It begins with a prince kissing
an angel. It ends with a baldheaded
man looking across the table at
a fat woman."
ANONYMOUS

"Marriage is the alliance of two people,
one of whom never remembers birthdays
and the other never forgets them."
OGDEN NASH (1902-1971)

Marriage halves our griefs, doubles our joys, and quadruples our expenses.

ENGLISH PROVERB

"When two people are under the influence of the most violent, most insane, most delusive, and most transient of passions, they are required to swear that they will remain in that excited, abnormal, and exhausting condition continuously until death do them part."

GEORGE BERNARD SHAW (1856-1950)

"I figure that the degree of difficulty in combining two lives ranks somewhere between rerouting a hurricane and finding a parking place in downtown Manhattan."

CLAIRE CLONINGER,
from "When the Glass Slipper Doesn't Fit and the Silver Spoon is in Someone Else's Mouth"

"Strange to say what delight we married people have to see these poor fools decoyed into our condition."

SAMUEL PEPYS (1633-1703)

"Though marriage makes man and wife one flesh, it leaves 'em still two fools."
WILLIAM CONGREVE (1670-1729)

The men that women marry,
And why they marry them, will always be
A marvel and a mystery to the world.
HENRY WADSWORTH LONGFELLOW (1807-1882)

"I tended to place my wife under a pedestal."
WOODY ALLEN

"The happy married man dies in good style at home, surrounded by his weeping wife and children. The old bachelor don't die at all – he sort of rots away, like a pollywog's tail."
ARTEMUS WARD (1834-1867)

"Love is looking over on the divan and discovering he's still lying there after sixteen years."
ANONYMOUS

"A successful marriage is not a gift; it is
an achievement."
ANN LANDERS, b.1918

"To live in love is life's greatest challenge.
It requires more subtlety, flexibility,
sensitivity, understanding, acceptance,
tolerance, knowledge and strength than
any other human endeavor or emotion."
LEO BUSCAGLIA

"In a successful marriage, there is no
such thing as one's way.
There is only the way of both, only
the bumpy, dusty, difficult, but always
mutual path!"
PHYLLIS McGINLEY

"A marriage where not only esteem, but
passion is kept awake, I am convinced,
the most perfect state of sublunary
happiness: but it requires great care to
keep this tender plant alive."
FRANCES BROOKE

"Perfect love is rare indeed....
To be a lover will require that you
continually have the subtlety of the
very wise, the flexibility of the child,
the sensitivity of the artist, the
understanding of the philosopher, the
acceptance of the saint, the tolerance of the
scholar, and the fortitude of the certain.
A tall order!"
LEO BUSCAGLIA

To keep your marriage brimming,
With love in the loving cup,
Whenever you're wrong, admit it;
Whenever you're right, shut up.

OGDEN NASH (1902-1971)

"Never forget the nine most important
words of any marriage:
1. I love you.
2. You are beautiful.
3. Please forgive me."

H. JACKSON BROWN, JR.

"'The last word' is the most dangerous
of infernal machines, and the
husband and wife should no
more fight to get it than they would
struggle for the possession of a
lighted bombshell."

DOUGLAS JERROLD (1803-1857)

"A happy marriage is the union of two
good forgivers."

RUTH BELL GRAHAM

"There is nothing nobler or more admirable than when two people who see eye to eye keep house as man and wife, confounding their enemies and delighting their friends."

HOMER (c.700 B.C.)

"Marriage has in it less of beauty, but more of safety, than the single life; it hath not more ease, but less danger; it is more merry and more sad; it is fuller of sorrows and fuller of joys; it lies under more burdens, but is supported by all the strengths of love and charity; and those burdens are delightful. Marriage is the mother of the world, and preserves kingdoms, and fills cities and churches, and heaven itself."

JEREMY TAYLOR (1613-1667)

"Any marriage, happy or unhappy, is infinitely more interesting and significant than any romance, however passionate."

W.H. AUDEN (1907-1973)

"Falling in love
is easy.
Growing in love
must be
worked at with
determination."
LESLEY BARFOOT

"Intensity of attraction is a beautiful thing.
But to mislabel it love is both foolish and
dangerous. What love requires on top of
instant emotion is time, shared experiences
and feelings, and a long and tempered
bond between two people."
STANTON PEELE

"Anything, everything, little or big
becomes an adventure when the right
person shares it."
KATHLEEN NORRIS (1880-1966)

"A good marriage is passion and
monotony, practicalities, magic, talk and
tears and laughter.
And at the core lies a place of trust
and love and deep content."
PAM BROWN, b.1928

"... that biggest blessing of loving
and being loved by those I loved and
respected; on earth no enjoyment
certainly to be put in the
balance with it."
RACHEL RUSSELL (1636-1723),
from a letter to the Earl of Galway

"To be content in bliss, without desire or
insistence anywhere, this was heaven: to
be together in happy stillness."
D.H. LAWRENCE (1885-1930)

"People are like vines....
We are born and we grow.
Like vines, people also need a tree to
cling to, to give them support."
ELIZABETH KATA

"Love is an act of endless forgiveness,
a tender look which
becomes a habit."
PETER USTINOV, b.1921

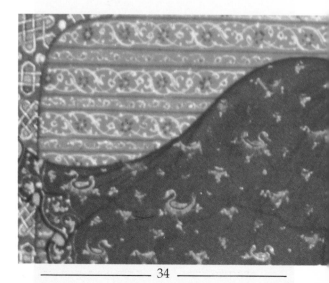

"I know some good marriages – marriages
where both people are just trying to
get through their days by helping
each other and being good to
each other."
ERICA JONG, b.1942

"Love is a willingness both to place
demands upon and receive demands from
another person."
DAVID G. JONES

"Kindness is the life's blood, the elixir of marriage. Kindness makes the difference between passion and caring. Kindness is tenderness. Kindness is love, but perhaps greater than love.... Kindness is good will. Kindness says, 'I want you to be happy'."

RANDOLPH RAY,
from "My Little Church around the Corner"

"It is a lovely thing to have a husband and wife developing together.
That is what marriage really means: helping one another to reach the full status of being persons, responsible and autonomous beings who do not run away from life."

PAUL TOURNIER

"Connubial happiness is a thing of too fine a texture to be handled roughly. It is a sensitive plant, which will not bear even the touch of unkindness; a delicate flower, which indifference will chill and suspicion blast."

THOMAS SPRAT (1636-1713)

"If there's something you need to say to your loved one, remember to say it lovingly, as if holding his heart in your hands."

ELLEN SUE STERN

"... We trade the newness for comfort.
For the deep, sustaining pleasure of not
having to put on a show, secure in
knowing that we are loved and accepted
for who we *really* are."

ELLEN SUE STERN

"That quiet mutual gaze of a trusting
husband and wife is like the first moment
of rest or refuge from a great weariness or
a great danger."

GEORGE ELIOT (MARY ANN EVANS) (1819-1880)

"A good marriage, if such there be, rejects
the company and conditions of love.
It tries to reproduce those of friendship.
It is a sweet association in life, full of
constancy, trust, and an infinite number
of useful and solid services and
mutual obligations."

MICHEL DE MONTAIGNE (1533-1592)

"The one word that makes a partnership
successful is 'OURS'."

JOANNE FINK

Let there be spaces in your
togetherness.
KAHLIL GIBRAN (1883-1931)

"Don't smother each other. No one can
grow in shade."
LEO BUSCAGLIA

"A good marriage is one which
allows for change and growth in
the individuals."
PEARL BUCK (1892-1973)

"Marriage must constantly fight
against a monster which devours
everything: routine."
HONORE DE BALZAC (1799-1850)

"... Then we can experience one of the
great gifts of marriage, which is the
degree to which we rouse each other to
dream dreams, to learn and grow and
reach for all life holds."
ELLEN SUE STERN

"After a few years of marriage, a man can look right at a woman without seeing her – and a woman can see right through a man without looking at him."

HELEN ROWLAND (1876-1950)

"No married man's ever made up his mind till he's heard what his wife has got to say about it."
W. SOMERSET MAUGHAM (1874-1965)

"Any married man should forget his mistakes – no use two people remembering the same thing."
DUANE DEWEL

"The concern that some women show at the absence of their husbands, does not arise from their not seeing them and being with them, but from their apprehension that their husbands are enjoying pleasures in which they do not participate, and which, from their being at a distance, they have not the power of interrupting."
MICHEL DE MONTAIGNE (1533-1592)

"Why does a woman work ten years to change a man's habits and then complain that he's not the man she married?"
BARBRA STREISAND, b.1942

"Marriage is nature's way of keeping people from fighting with strangers."
ALAN KING, b.1927

"Holy Deadlock."
A.P. HERBERT (1890-1971)
title of novel

"On their wedding anniversary, my young brother sent our parents a card. In it he wrote: 'To Mum and Dad. Fifteen years of married Blitz!'"
MRS L.M. HOPE

"Then marriage may be said to be past in all quietnesse, when the wife is blind, and the husband deafe."
THOMAS HEYWOOD (c. 1574-1641),
from "Dialogues"

"A woman knows there are two sides to every question: there is her husband's side and there is the right side."
ANONYMOUS

"My husband will never chase
another woman. He's too fine, too
decent, too old."
GRACIE ALLEN

"When he is late for dinner and I know
he must be either having an affair or
lying dead in the street, I always
hope he's dead."
JUDITH VIORST

"When a man opens the car door
for his wife, it's either a new car
or a new wife."
PRINCE PHILIP, b.1921

"Marriage: A legal or religious
ceremony by which two persons
of the opposite sex solemnly agree
to harass and spy on each other
for ninety-nine years, or until death do
them join."
ELBERT HUBBARD (1865-1915)

"Marriage is a serious business, but love
turns the grey of life to gold."
MIRIAM OSBORNE

"A real marriage bears no resemblance
to these marriages of interest or
ambition. It is two lovers who
live together."
LADY MARY WORTLEY MONTAGU (1689-1762)

"Those who love deeply never grow
old; they may die of old age, but
they die young."
ARTHUR WING PINERO

"Love and marriage, love and marriage,
Go together like a horse and carriage."
SAMMY CAHN, b.1913

"Why get married if not to enjoy
the pleasure of having another human
being treat us as if we are God's gift
to humanity?"
ELLEN SUE STERN

"Clym and Eustacia, in their little house at Alderworth, were living on with a monotony which was delightful to them. The heath and changes of weather were quite blotted out from their eyes for the present.... When it rained they were charmed, because they could remain indoors together all day with such a show of reason; when it was fine they were charmed, because they could sit together on the hills..."

THOMAS HARDY (1840-1928), *from "The Return of the Native"*

"You can tell a good, surviving marriage by the expression in the partners' eyes – like those of sailors who have shared the battles against foul weather – and the scented airs of summer at sea.
They welcome visitors – but are content with their own company."

PAM BROWN, b.1928

"Throughout our years together, we had built up history and a closeness so subtle we didn't even know it was there."

ERMA BOMBECK, b. 1927

"Stirring the oatmeal is a humble act... it represents a willingness to find meaning in the simple unromantic tasks: earning a living, living within a budget, putting out the garbage."

ROBERT A. JOHNSON

"True love is...
... sharing your teddy
... giving away your last licorice allsort
... someone who thinks you are beautiful
even with your teeth out
... being able to laugh at the same jokes
again and again and again
... a listening ear, a caressing eye
holding hands and wanting to cry
... boiling cauliflower when you're pregnant
... sharing a grape"

GILL DAVIES

"The happiness of married life depends
upon making small sacrifices with
readiness and cheerfulness."

JOHN SELDEN (1584-1654)

"It doesn't take much: a shared shower in
the morning, a sexy message on his
answering machine at work, a little note in
his lunchbox, a long hug before we turn
off the lights. These are the little-things-
that-go-a-long-way."

ELLEN SUE STERN

Remember you the trails and
forest we walked, with hands
Joined, and our heads leaning
against each other, as if
We were hiding within ourselves?
KAHLIL GIBRAN (1883-1931)

"Nothing can match the treasure of
common memories...."
ANTOINE DE SAINT-EXUPERY (1900-1944)

"The sum which two married people owe
to one another defies calculation.
It is an infinite debt, which can only be
discharged through eternity."
JOHANN WOLFGANG VON GOETHE (1749-1832)

"Love is absolute loyalty. People fade,
looks fade, but loyalty never fades."
SYLVESTER STALLONE

"The love we have in our youth is
superficial compared to the love that an
old man has for his wife."
WILL DURANT

"One of the good things that come of
a true marriage is, that there is one face
on which changes come without your
seeing them; or rather there is one face
which you can still see the same, through
all the shadows which years have
gathered upon it."

GEORGE MACDONALD (1824-1905)

Until you're a hundred,
Until I'm ninety-nine,
Together
Until white hair grows

JAPANESE FOLK SONG

"Two persons who have chosen each other
out of all the species, with the design to be
each other's mutual comfort and
entertainment, have, in that action, bound
themselves to be good-humoured, affable,
discreet, forgiving, patient, and joyful,
with respect to each other's frailties
and perfections, to the end of their lives."

JOSEPH ADDISON (1672-1719)

"A happy marriage is a long conversation
that always seems too short."

ANDRE MAUROIS (1885-1967)

"Love seems the swiftest but it is
the slowest of all growths.
No man or woman really knows
what perfect love is until they have
been married a quarter
of a century."

MARK TWAIN (1835-1910)

"We should measure affection not
like youngsters, by the ardour of
its passion, but by its strength and
constancy."

CICERO (106-43 B.C.)

"... To have and to hold from this
day forward, for better for worse,
for richer for poorer, in sickness and
in health, to love and to cherish,
till death do us part...."

from The Book of Common Prayer

"Marriage... notwithstanding all the loose talk of the town, the satires of ancient, or modern pretenders to wit, will never lose its just esteem from the wise and good."

MARY ASTELL, *from "Reflections Upon Marriage", 1700*

"Marriage is the proper remedy. It is the most natural state of man, and therefore the state in which you are most likely to find solid happiness."

BENJAMIN FRANKLIN (1706-1790)

"The institution of marriage keeps the moral world in being, and secures it from an untimely dissolution. Without it, natural affection and amiableness would not exist, domestic education would become extinct, industry and economy be unknown, and man would be left to the precarious existence of the savage."

TIMOTHY DWIGHT (1752-1817)

"The married state, with the affection suitable to it, is the completest image of heaven and hell we are capable of receiving in this life."

RICHARD STEELE

"And when will there be an end of marrying? I suppose, when there is an end of living!"

TERTULLIAN (c. 160-220)